From Past to PRESEN

A History of Time

by Paul Bennett

GARETH STEVENS
GS
PUBLISHING
A Member of the WRC Media Family of Companies

Please visit our web site at: www.garethstevens.com
For a free color catalog describing Gareth Stevens Publishing's list of high-quality books and multimedia programs, call 1-800-542-2595 (USA) or 1-800-387-3178 (Canada). Gareth Stevens Publishing's fax: (414) 332-3567.

Library of Congress Cataloging-in-Publication Data

Bennett, Paul, 1954-
A history of time / Paul Bennett. — North American ed.
p. cm. — (From past to present)
Includes index.
ISBN 0-8368-6289-9 (lib. bdg.)
1. Time—History—Popular works. 2. Time measurements—History—Popular works. I. Title. II. Series.
QB209.B458 2006
529'.709—dc22 2005054081

This North American edition first published in 2006 by
Gareth Stevens Publishing
A Member of the WRC Media Family of Companies
330 West Olive Street, Suite 100
Milwaukee, WI 53212 USA

Gareth Stevens editor: Leifa Butrick
Gareth Stevens designer: Kami M. Strunsee

The publishers would like to thank Graham Rich, Rosalind Beckman, and Elizabeth Wiggans for their assistance.

Picture credits: (t=top, b=bottom, c=center, l=left, r=right)
AKG Photo: 11t, 15tr, 15tl, 19b, 19cl, 18c. All Sports Photo/Mike Powell: 21cr. Ann Ronan@Image Select: 5cl, 5cr, 12b, 13c, 16b, 19t, 23br. Ann Ronan Picture Library: 8c, 10rc, 13t. Art Archive: 30c. Bridgemann Art Library: 13bl, 13br. Breitling: cover, 20c. Colorific: 23bl, 33c. CFCL@Image Select: 15c, 19tr, 21t, 28t. e.t. archive: 8b. FPG International: 28c. Image Select: 10b. J.Allan Cash Ltd: 7c, 15br, 17bl. John Frost: 27t. Jean Loup Charmet: 17cr. Mary Evans Picture Library: 14b, 17bl, 17tr, 24bl. National Maritime Museum Library: 18b, 22b, 24br, 24c. National Portrait Gallery, London: 27cr. Natural History Museum, London: 6cl. Planet Earth Pictures: 6cr, 7tr, 26c, 26bl, 28b, 31b, 31c. PIX S.A.: 7tl, 9cl. Popperfoto: 27b. Rex Features, London: 23tl, 25tl, 26br. Science Photo Library: 7b, 12c, 21cr, 29b, 29t, 30b, 31t, 31c, 33b. Sony: 23tr. Telegraph Colour Picture Library UK: 5b, 4c, 6cr, 6b, 9t, 9br, 11b, 14c, 17br, 19cr, 21b, 20b, 23c, 25tr, 27cl. The Kobal Collection: 29c, 33b. The Stock Market: 4b. ticktock Entertainment Ltd. 5b, 25c, 32r. Tony Stone: 5tl, 9cr 15bl, 22c. University College London: 32l. Werner Forman Archive: 16c.

Printed in the United States of America

1 2 3 4 5 6 7 8 9 10 09 08 07 06

CONTENTS

Words that appear in the glossary are printed in **boldface** type the first time they occur in the text.

What Is Time?

When you wake up in the morning, one of your first thoughts is probably, "What time is it?" You look at your clock to know whether you can go back to sleep or whether you should get out of bed. All through the day, you will be aware of time. You may look at your watch or a clock, and, from what it tells you, you will know if it is time for lunch, time to meet a friend, or time for a favorite TV program. In fact, our lives are so ruled by time that it is hard to imagine living a whole day without keeping track of it. Time helps us put order into our days. It tells us what we should be doing or when something will happen. Time is like a never-ending river carrying us along, moving us from the past to the present and on to the future. Time is the map of our lives.

Becoming Aware of Time

Babies do not know how to tell time. They live moment by moment. When they feel hungry, they cry for food. When they are tired, they sleep. They may be ready to play in the middle of the night. During their first few years, they become aware of certain things that happen every day. From their daily schedules, they gradually learn when it is time for meals and bed. In the early school years, they learn to read a clock. Nearly everything that happens at home and at school will be organized by time. Soon, telling time seems the most natural thing in the world.

Family Ties

This picture shows three **generations** of a family — children, parents, and grandparents. "Generation" is another way of describing time. A generation is a step in a family tree. It is the time it takes for children to grow up and become parents themselves. Genealogists study family ties and how people are related through the generations.

Remembering Special Days

Calendars and diaries divide a year up into days, weeks, and months. They also note religious festivals, national holidays, and other special days. Many of these important days happen on the same date each year, such as Halloween, which is always on October 31. We use calendars to remind us of important events in our lives, such as birthdays and anniversaries, and diaries help us remember the past.

Time Ticking Away

The White Rabbit from *Alice's Adventures in Wonderland* is famous for taking a watch out of his waistcoat pocket and muttering to himself, "Oh dear! Oh dear! I shall be too late!" Just like us, he is aware of the passing of time. Using watches, we can split up time into tiny bits. Watches can measure seconds — even fractions of seconds — minutes, and hours.

Out with the Old, In with the New

Old Father Time is seen here carrying the New Year on his shoulders. Time is often represented as an old man, and, because the New Year represents new beginnings, it often is depicted as a young child.

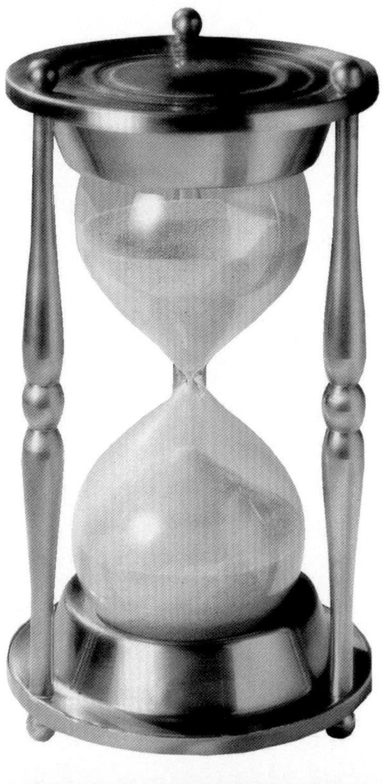

The Sands of Time

The phrase "the sands of time" comes from the **hourglass,** which was used to measure hours. In an hourglass, the sand trickles from one glass bulb to another through a narrow hole between the two. When all the sand has trickled through, that amount of time has passed. Then the hourglass can be turned over to measure additional time. A familiar saying, "The sands are running out," means that time is nearly up. Small timers filled with sand, which cooks use to measure just a few minutes, are cousins of the hourglass.

Body Clocks

Before watches and clocks were invented, people were not as concerned with keeping track of time. Their built-in sense of time, a kind of basic rhythm, helped them live in tune with events in the world around them, such as the rising and setting of the Sun and the changing seasons. We still have these built-in "clocks" in our bodies today. Scientists have discovered that our patterns of waking and sleeping follow something they call "**circadian rhythm**," a rhythm that is affected by the amount of daylight and darkness in our lives. Experiments have shown that people's **body clocks** are about twenty-five hours long. Many other living things have their own body clocks, too. Lizards and snakes move slowly early in the morning. As they warm themselves in the Sun, they become more active.

Natural Time

Early humans did not look at time the way we do. They were not aware of seconds, minutes, and hours. They awoke at sunrise, and, while it was light, they hunted animals, gathered plants for food, and made tools and shelters. They knew from experience what different creatures would be doing during the day, such as feeding or resting, and which plants would have fruit. Their circadian rhythm supported their survival, prompting them to use daylight hours effectively.

Monsters of the Deep

Some animals live in underground caves or in the deep sea and never see sunlight. Although they don't know about day and night, they have their own body rhythms to ensure their survival. They know when to eat, sleep, and mate. This weird-looking fish is a fangtooth, and it lives in the deepest part of the ocean. Its body is covered with prickly scales. Because of its menacing appearance, it is nicknamed "ogrefish," but it is only 6 inches (15 centimeters) long.

Plankton

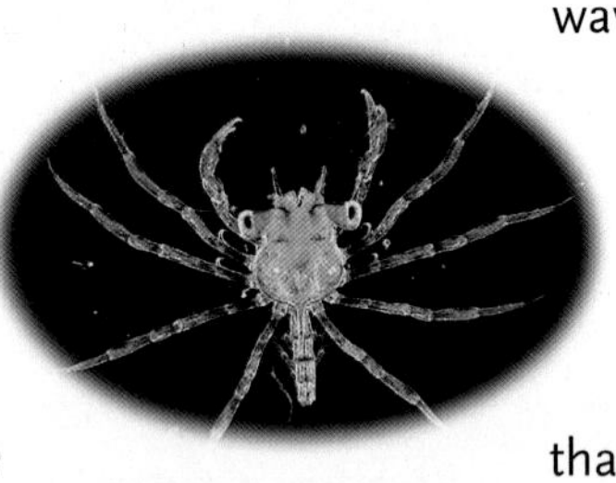

Even the smallest creatures have body clocks. Plankton are small, drifting animals that live in the oceans. In the daytime, they stay a few hundred feet (meters) below the waves to avoid being eaten. As the Sun goes down, they move up to the surface of the sea to feed on the many algae that grow there. They often form enormous "blooms" that color the water green.

The Tides

The Moon's gravity and, to a lesser extent, that of the Sun cause a rhythmic, twice-daily rising and falling of the tides. Scientists have noticed that circadian rhythm and the rhythm of the tides (every twenty-four hours and fifty minutes) are very similar. Some people believe that this similarity came about because we evolved from creatures that lived in the oceans millions of years ago. Perhaps we have a kind of ancient memory that makes our body clocks tick today.

Night Shift

The body clocks of creatures vary even among the same types of animals. Many birds, for example, sing during the day, but owls hoot at night. Just as daytime creatures are settling down for the night, nighttime creatures are on the move, on the lookout for a tasty meal. Mice, bats, and many insects wake up when the Sun goes down, and their senses are specially adapted to allow them to see their dimly lit world just as clearly as we can see ours during the day.

Plant Rhythms

Plants have their own natural rhythms, too. Many flowers open and close according to how much sunlight there is. On a dark, cloudy day, some flowers may not open much at all. Some plants, such as sunflowers, follow the movement of the Sun across the sky because they need its light for growth. When they are ready, flowers produce seeds, which fall to the ground and grow into new plants the next year.

The Midnight Sun

Near the North Pole, the Sun never sets in summer. There are twenty-four hours of daylight, and countries, such as Greenland (*shown right*) that fringe the Arctic Circle are called the Land of the Midnight Sun. Many people do not adjust well to the long hours of daylight in the Arctic. Their circadian rhythm becomes upset, their sleep suffers, and they feel tired and irritable.

Since the earliest times, people observed the patterns of the world around them: the regular appearances of the Sun and Moon in the sky, the annual changes in temperature and climate, the growth each year of trees and other plants, and the movements of animals. From these observations, they decided to divide the year into periods with particular weather conditions — spring, summer, autumn, and winter — and to use "nature's clock" to plan for the future. Farmers recognized the right time of year to sow seeds or to harvest crops, and they also knew when animals made their annual **migrations**. Until five hundred years ago, no one understood why we have seasons. They were simply thought to be part of God's great plan and were not questioned. We now know, scientifically, that we have seasons because of the way Earth rotates around the Sun.

The Seasons and the Solar Year

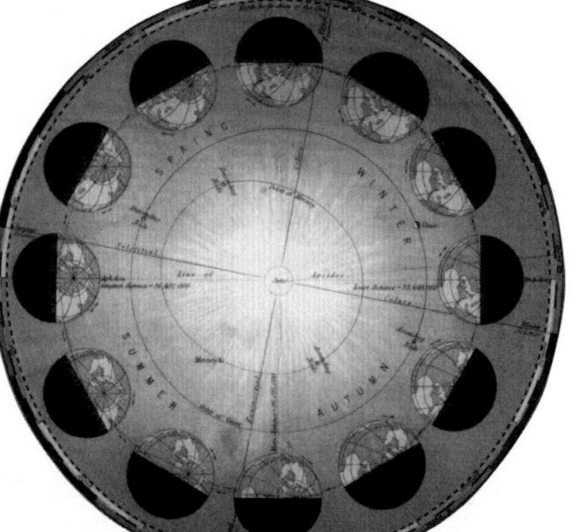

The movement of Earth around the Sun causes the seasons. This picture (*right*) shows Earth's path around the Sun. Earth's axis is not perfectly upright. It is always tilted slightly. As Earth moves around the Sun, different parts of the surface of Earth lean toward the Sun and get more sunlight. For some months of the year, the North Pole is tilted toward the Sun, and the South Pole is tilted away from the Sun. During this time, the Northern Hemisphere has the long, warm days of summer, while the Southern Hemisphere has the short, cold days of winter. Later in the year, when the South Pole is tilted toward the Sun and the North Pole is tilted away from it, the seasons in the Northern and Southern hemispheres are reversed. The **solar year** is approximately 365¼ days long.

Harvest Time

As summer ends, farmers harvest their crops. Traditionally, the end of summer is an important time, for, if there is a good harvest, people will have plenty of food for the cold winter months when nothing is growing. A good harvest also provides seeds for growing crops the following spring.

Migration

The spectacular migrations of animals are linked to the seasons and the availability of food. In the African dry season, for example, when all the grass has been eaten in the northern countries, hundreds of thousands of wildebeests march south, crossing deep rivers that may be on their way, to find new places where grass is growing. The wildebeests migrate north again when fresh grass grows there after the rains.

Seasonal Cycles in Plants

The cycle of seasons brings about obvious changes in plants. These changes are triggered by soil temperatures and the lengths of the days. **Perennial plants** (those that live for more than one year) have cycles for growing and shedding their leaves. The maple tree is a good example. When autumn approaches, its leaves are deprived of moisture and cannot form new chlorophyll. The green color disappears, and the leaves turn yellow and red. When the leaves turn brown and dry, they fall off.

Hibernation

The biological clocks of many animals are linked to the seasons. An internal "alarm" causes a change in behavior. In summer and autumn, animals such as groundhogs, raccoons, and chipmunks eat to build up a store of fat that will provide the energy they need while they are **hibernating**. During their winter sleep, their breathing and heartbeat slow down so they expend little energy and can survive the harsh winter months without food. When warmer weather arrives, they wake up and return to their summer activities.

Vacation Time

Because many people want to take advantage of particular weather conditions, their vacations may be affected by the seasons. In the cold winter months, sports such as skiing are popular. In the warmer summer months, people flock to beaches or the countryside. Long-distance travel, however, allows people to take vacations at the beach even in winter.

Long before there were clocks, people relied on regular, natural events to keep track of time. They worked, ate, and slept, for example, according to the rising and setting of the Sun. Thus, we now use the word *day* to describe not only the twenty-four hours from one midnight to the next, but also the period of light from sunrise to sunset. People long ago studied the four seasons, too, and, by keeping track of the Sun's position in the sky, they could mark the passing of one year and the start of another. The quiet winter period, when farmers prepared the ground for sowing seeds in the coming spring, became the natural end of the year. There was no other obvious measure between a day and a year, but many people used the phases of the Moon for further measurements of time.

The Egyptians

The earliest Egyptian calendars were based on the movements of the Moon and the annual flooding of the Nile River, which was welcomed as part of the annual cycle of the seasons. The level of the Nile still rises dramatically every year as a result of heavy summer rain falling on mountains to the south. The Nile overflows its banks and floods the land, leaving a layer of mud that enriches the soil and provides a strip of good farmland in the middle of the desert.

Egyptian Sky Goddess

Our ancestors observed the natural rhythms of the world around them and developed explanations for what was happening, which they often included in their religions. The people of Ancient Egypt, for example, believed that the sky was a goddess called Nut, who arched her body over Earth (*left*). They believed the Sun was a god called Ra. Every evening, Nut swallowed Ra, the setting Sun, and every morning, she gave birth to him again.

Aztec Calendar

By observing the natural world, the priests of early farming civilizations were able to make calendars that predicted the seasons. Early calendars, such as this one (*right*) carved in stone by the Aztec people of Central America, were often very elaborate. Archaeologists have discovered that the Sun played an important role in the religious life of many early civilizations and was worshipped as a god.

Sun Worship

In early times, the sky was believed to be the home of the gods who controlled the movement of the Sun, the changing phases of the Moon, and the seasons. Many cultures worshipped these gods. Astronomer-priests kept records of what they saw and looked for ways to honor the gods by building temples and carrying out rituals. Stonehenge (*below*) is one of Europe's most important temples. It was built in about 1800 B.C. and was aligned to receive the rays of the midsummer sunrise. Many people believe astronomer-priests used Stonehenge to predict the motions of the Sun and the Moon and when eclipses might occur.

The different ways of measuring time — days, months, and years — all worked reasonably well until people tried to put them together into one calendar. The problem was twofold: The number of days in a lunar month ($29^1/_2$ days) did not fit exactly into a solar year ($365^1/_4$ days), and the number of lunar months themselves did not fit into a solar year (twelve months, eleven days). Timekeeping became confused as the calendars fell out of step. The early Romans, for example, adopted a system of ten months in a year, but, eventually, the months that were supposed to come in winter fell in autumn. To solve the problem, the Romans added extra days and months when they needed them. By 46 B.C., the system was such a mess that Roman general Julius Caesar reformed the calendar. The Roman calendar then became known as the **Julian calendar**, and it lasted for the next 1,600 years.

The Lunar Month

Just as Earth travels around the Sun, the Moon travels around Earth. Each orbit takes about $29^1/_2$ days and the time is called a **lunar month**. This diagram (*left*), with the Sun at the top and Earth at the center (*blue*), shows the phases of the Moon during each lunar month. The orbit of the Moon is shown twice. The inner ring (*red is the far side of the Moon, never seen from Earth*) shows the reflection of the Sun's rays on the Moon while the other half is in shadow. The outer ring shows what the Moon actually looks like from Earth in its different phases. The new Moon, at the top, is not visible from Earth because the Sun's light falls on its far side.

The Chinese Calendar

The Chinese year is not the same number of days long as the solar year. It is measured in lunar months, and an extra month is added at regular intervals to keep the months within their proper seasons. The Chinese named their years after twelve animals, and the years repeat in a cycle that starts with the Year of the Rat, followed by the Years of the Ox, Tiger, Rabbit, Dragon, Snake, Horse, Ram, Monkey, Cock, Dog, and Pig. The particular personality characteristics of each animal are believed to pass on to people born that year, so people born in the Year of the Rabbit, for example, will be happy and content and blessed with large families.

Days of the Week

Seven does not fit exactly into 365 days or 366 days, so why do we have a week made up of seven days? One answer is that the Romans believed seven was a lucky number. They also saw seven objects in the sky that did not move with the stars: the Sun, the Moon, and the planets Mars, Mercury, Jupiter, Venus, and Saturn. These names, together with names of Norse and Anglo-Saxon gods, greatly influenced the names for the days of the week.

Day	Origin of Name
Sunday	The Sun
Monday	The Moon
Tuesday	Twi, Norse god of war and the sky
Wednesday	Woden, chief Anglo-Saxon god
Thursday	Thor, Norse god of thunder (*shown left*, wielding his mighty hammer)
Friday	Frigga, Anglo-Saxon goddess of the heavens and wife of Woden
Saturday	Saturn, Roman god of agriculture

The Julian Calendar

Julius Caesar's reforms corrected the problems with the Roman calendar. He introduced a year made up of twelve unequal months, seven of them having thirty-one days, four having thirty days, and one with twenty-eight days (making 365 days). Every fourth year, an extra day was added to February because a solar year is a few hours longer than 365 days. The fourth year is called a **leap year**. The Julian calendar abandoned any connection with the phases

Earth-Centered Universe

For thousands of years, astronomers believed that Earth was the center of the universe and that the Sun, Moon, planets, and a huge sphere to which the stars were attached all circled Earth. This was the Ptolemaic system, named after the Greek astronomer Ptolemy (85-165 A.D.), whose theories ruled the world of astronomy for 1,500 years.

Nicolaus Copernicus

The idea of an Earth-centered universe was supported by the Christian Church, which said that God had created a universe with Earth at its heart. In 1543, Polish astronomer Nicolaus Copernicus (*right*) published a book that said the Sun, not Earth, was at the center of the system of planets and stars. Copernicus's ideas changed our view of the cosmos.

The Julian calendar was a great success. Finally, people had a calendar that matched the solar year — or so everyone thought. The solar year, however, is not exactly 365¼ days long. It is shorter by eleven minutes and fourteen seconds. This amount of time may seem tiny compared to a whole year, but over 128 years, it resulted in the loss of one full day. By the year 1580, more than sixteen hundred years after the Julian calendar had been introduced, the calendar was wrong by ten days. Pope Gregory XIII was greatly concerned about this loss of days because calculating the date of Easter was becoming difficult, and Easter was drifting slowly back toward Christmas. Pope Gregory consulted his astronomers, who calculated the actual length of the solar year and provided the basis of our modern calendar, known as the Gregorian calendar.

The Modern Calendar

The calendar we use today is called the Gregorian calendar, named after the Pope who introduced it in 1582. To correct the "missing" ten days, Pope Gregory XIII ordered that the day after October 4 that year would be October 15. This did not, however, solve the whole problem because a new error would slowly build up and another ten days would be lost again over sixteen hundred years. Pope Gregory's solution was to have a calendar with three fewer leap years every four hundred years. Thus, the years 1700, 1800, and 1900 were not leap years, but the year 2000 was. Even this calendar is not perfect. In about three thousand years, there will be another "missing" day. Today, all the countries of the world use the Gregorian calendar for official purposes.

By Common Consent

The Gregorian calendar was calculated from the year that Christians believe Jesus Christ was born. The years before Christ's birth are B.C. (before Christ) and the years after are A.D. (*Anno Domini,* Latin for "year of our Lord"). The Jewish religious calendar dates from when Jews believe the world was created, and the Muslim calendar from when Muhammad moved to Medina. In recognition of the differing traditions, the letters B.C.E. (before the common era) and C.E. (common era) are sometimes used instead of the Christian B.C. and A.D.

The Muslim Year

The Muslim calendar is based on the position and movement of the Moon. It has twelve calendar months, which are either twenty-nine or thirty days long, making the Islamic year shorter than the Christian year. Unlike the Christian day, the Muslim day starts and ends at sunset. The picture above shows a procession at the end of the Muslim festival of Ramadan, which lasts one lunar month.

Hindu Festivals

Because the phases of the Moon dictate Hindu festivals, their dates change from year to year. This girl (*right*) is celebrating Diwali, the Hindu festival of lights, which falls in the autumn month of October or November. Small lamps are lit every night of this four-day celebration to symbolize the power of goodness over the forces of darkness.

The Jewish Calendar

Because the Jewish calendar is based on the movements of the Moon, important dates in the Jewish religion vary from year to year. The Jewish New Year occurs in September or October, and the festival of Passover, which is being celebrated in the picture above, falls in March or April. The Jewish calendar has twelve months. A Jewish leap year has one extra month.

George Washington's Birthday

At first, not everyone accepted the new Gregorian calendar. It was used mostly by countries that observed the Catholic religion. When George Washington, the first president of the United States (1732–1799), was born, the American colonies observed the Protestant religions and still used the Julian calendar. Washington was born on February 11, but according to our current Gregorian calendar, and taking into account the missing days, his birthday is February 22.

Chinese New Year

All around the world, a new year officially begins on January 1. Many countries, however, still use calendars based on the movements of the Moon. The Chinese New Year, for example, begins on the first day of the lunar year —the day of the new Moon in late January or early February. It is celebrated with colorful processions and fireworks.

Using the Elements of Timekeeping

The Ancient Egyptians were the first people to divide a day into twenty-four hours. They divided the night into twelve parts, based on the regular movements of the stars across the heavens. As a particular star rose in the night sky, they knew an hour had passed and another one was about to start. They decided to divide the day into twelve equal parts, too, but during the hours of daylight, they could not see the stars. To solve the problem, they used the movement of the Sun and the shadow that a sundial casts to keep track of time. Later, the hours were divided up into smaller and smaller units — minutes and seconds, with sixty seconds in a minute and sixty minutes in an hour. The Babylonians are believed to be the first civilization to use sixty as a base for calculating large numbers, so the way we divide hours into minutes and minutes into seconds may have been influenced by Babylonian culture.

Sundials

On a sundial, a pointer, called a gnomon, casts a shadow onto a flat base. The base is marked with a scale to show the hours of the day. As the position of the Sun changes in the sky, the shadow from the gnomon changes, too, and shows the time on the scale. This sundial (*right*) is from the Forbidden City in China.

Seasons and Shadows

Shadows cast by the Sun change in length as well as in direction. The shadows are longest in the morning and evening, when the Sun is low on the horizon, and shortest at midday, when the Sun is overhead. The seasons of the year, as well as time, can be determined from the lengths of shadows. In summer, the Sun is higher in the sky than in winter. These tribesmen in Borneo (*left*) are measuring the length of a shadow cast by a stick planted in the ground. They always measure the shadow at midday so they can tell how the seasons are changing.

Time Trickling Away

The **clepsydra** is a water-filled vessel used to measure time. It has a hole in the base, through which water drains away. The Egyptians used clepsydras more than twenty-five hundred years ago. Some are marked with lines that relate to the twelve hours of the night. The bowl (*right*) is a clepsydra from southern India. When it is full, the attendant will ring the triangle to let people know that a certain amount of time has passed.

Chinese Water Clock

This Chinese clepsydra has containers set at different levels, forming a kind of staircase down which water flows. When all the water reaches the bottom container, the timekeeper records the time, carries the water to the top, and starts the process again.

Ship's Bell

In the past, mariners rang a bell to signal half-hour intervals on ships. At sea, the day was broken up into six four-hour periods called watches, and a member of the crew rang the bell while on watch.

Candle Power

From the front, this clock (*right*) looks similar to the clocks we know today. This unusual French invention, however, is a candlestick with a clock face that has a glass dial and single hand. The hand is moved by a chain attached to a spring, which, in turn, is connected to the base of the candle. As the candle burns, the hand moves around the clock face.

Candle Clock

For many centuries, candle clocks were used to keep track of time. Some historians believe they were invented by the English king Alfred the Great, in the ninth century. The candle often was divided into sections that each took one hour to burn.

Mechanical Clocks

Until about six hundred years ago, sundials were the most popular way to measure time. Some people had mechanical clocks, but these clocks had bells instead of hands to tell time and often were not accurate. The word *clock* probably comes from *clocca*, the Latin word for bell. The 1650s saw a great breakthrough in clock making when Dutch scientist Christiaan Huygens built the first pendulum clock. A pendulum is a weight swinging from a fixed point. Huygens realized that the regular swing of the pendulum would be perfect for measuring time accurately. All mechanical clocks need a way to move their hands at an even speed, and Huygens found a way to link the pendulum's swing to a mechanism that moved a clock's hands in regular ticks.

Galileo's Discovery

In the 1580s, Galileo, an Italian mathematician and astronomer, discovered how a pendulum worked. While sitting in Pisa Cathedral, he watched the swing of a hanging lamp, measuring the time it took to make a complete swing and discovering that it took the same amount of time even when the size of the swing changed. Galileo applied his observations to experiments with pendulums but never made a pendulum clock.

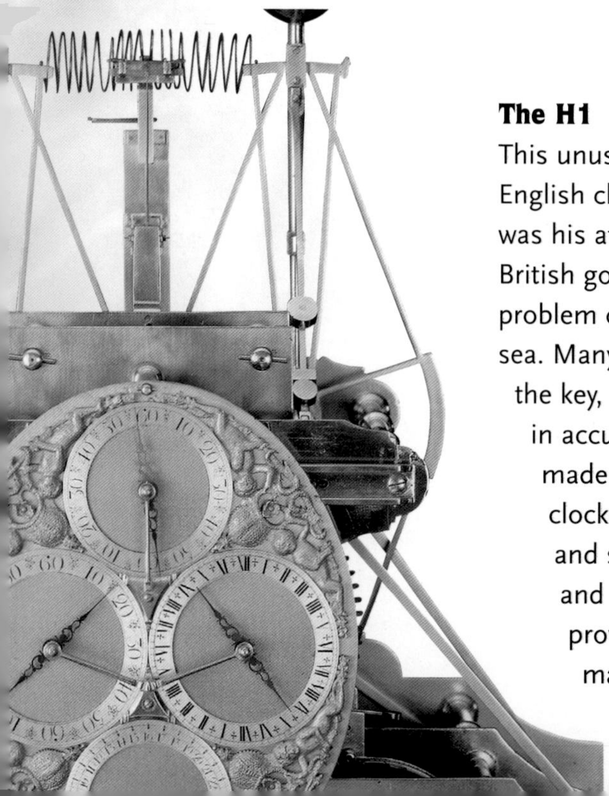

The H1

This unusual looking clock is the invention of English clock maker John Harrison (1693–1776). It was his attempt to win a cash prize offered by the British government to anyone who could solve the problem of how to determine a ship's position at sea. Many people thought studying the stars was the key, but Harrison proved that the solution lay in accurate timekeeping. The rolling of the ship made pendulum clocks unworkable. Harrison's clock, called the H1, had a new mechanism and separate dials for seconds, minutes, hours, and days of the month. Although the clock proved to work very well, Harrison wanted to make a clock that was smaller and even more accurate.

Christiaan Huygens

Dutch scientist Christiaan Huygens revolutionized timekeeping when he built the first pendulum clock. He discovered that he could keep a pendulum swinging if he attached a small weight to a reel. As the weight gradually fell, it pulled the reel around, which kept the pendulum swinging. Winding the weight with a key, once a day or once a week, lifted the weight to keep the pendulum going.

Keeping Time

Musicians use a **metronome** to keep time with the beat of the music. The metronome indicates the tempo of the music by producing a clicking sound from a swinging arm (the pendulum). A small, adjustable weight on the arm controls the speed of the swing. The higher the position of the weight, the slower the swing.

A Grandfather Clock

This ornate grandfather clock (*right*) was made in France in the eighteenth century. A grandfather clock has a falling weight that provides the energy to keep the pendulum swinging inside the clock. The weight is attached to a long chain so the clock will work for several days before it stops.

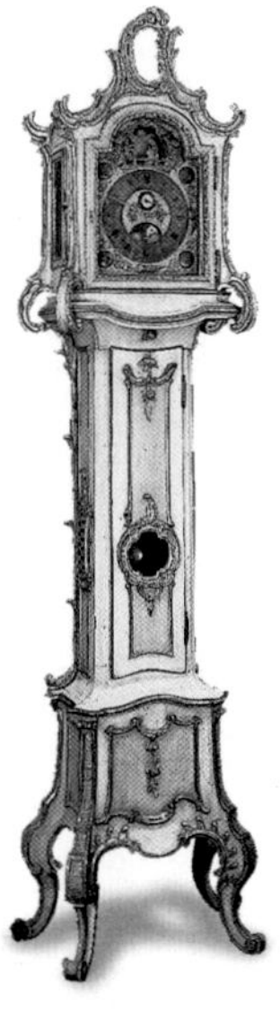

Big Ben

Big Ben is the name of the great bell in the clock tower of the Houses of Parliament in London. The clock, which has a 13-foot (4-meter) pendulum, is famous for its accuracy. Big Ben (*right*) first boomed out in 1859.

Grand Clocks

Large, public clocks are often very ornate. On this clock face, the twenty-four hours of the day are marked in Roman numerals on the outer ring. Inside the hours are the signs of the zodiac, representing the months or divisions of the year. Bells ring to let everyone know the time of day, even if they cannot see the clock.

Timekeeping in Today's World

Bang! Today, we have the means to reduce time to such a fine degree that we can photograph a bullet as it is shot from a gun. High-speed photography is just one of the benefits that have come from modern methods of keeping time. The incredibly tiny fractions of a second that can now be measured have helped scientists understand more about our world and the nature of the universe. In our everyday lives, we use watches that people just forty years ago would have been amazed to see. The revolution in the way we keep and use time started with the development of the quartz watch in the late 1960s. Quartz is a common mineral found in the ground. When a small current of electricity from a battery passes through quartz, the quartz vibrates an exact number of times per second. Microchips, like the ones found in computers, count the vibrations and display the time on the face of the watch.

Following Fashion

The wristwatch was invented by Patek Philippe at the end of the nineteenth century. It was considered a woman's accessory until Louis Cartier designed a leather-band wristwatch for an airplane pilot, who found it much handier than a pocket watch. Wristwatches became popular on the battlefields of World War I. Artillery and infantry officers had to **synchronize** watches to conduct attacks precisely, so inexpensive, reliable watches were issued routinely to officers, who were allowed to keep them when they were demobilized. Today, wristwatches come in many different styles.

Spring-Driven Mechanisms

In a mechanical watch, the pendulum and weight of the bulky grandfather clock have been replaced by tiny coiled springs. The springs drive the mechanism and regulate the speed of the wheels that turn the hands on the face of the watch. The spring-driven watch is one of the most precise mechanical objects ever made.

Digital Displays

Digital watches and clocks display time as digits, or numbers, unlike analog clocks, which display time with hands on a dial. The digital readout is made of a material called liquid crystal, which responds to electrical signals sent by the electronic counter in the watch.

Atomic Clocks

Atomic clocks are so incredibly accurate that they lose or gain no more than a second in two or three million years! These clocks use the energy changes that take place in atoms to keep track of time. This atomic clock (*right*) is the US NBS-4 atomic clock.

Photo Finish

Races are won and lost by hundredths of a second — finishes so close they would be impossible to judge using our eyes alone. A modern timing system for races relies on computers wired to a starter's gun and a timing camera at the finish line. When the gun goes off, the computer starts timing the athletes and, with the aid of the camera, captures precisely the moment each athlete crosses the finish line.

Speed of a Bullet

According to the Greek philosopher Zeno of Elea, a bullet would never hit a running man. If a man has a head start of 100 yards (90 meters) when a gun is fired and can run 1 yard (1 m) for every 100 yards (90 m) the bullet travels, when the bullet has flown 100 yards (90 m), the man has traveled 1 yard (1 m). By the time the bullet has traveled that extra distance, the man will have covered an additional 3.6 inches (9 centimeters). And so it continues. The distance becomes smaller, but the bullet never hits its target. Of course, Zeno's theory is nonsense. In real life, the bullet would hit the man because time does not stand still and cannot be chopped up into smaller and smaller pieces.

Throughout the day, we check our watches to see that we are on time for the next thing we have to do. Often, our busy schedules are set by others. Teachers at school must know when their classes start and finish, trains and planes need to run on time, and the times of TV programs are published well in advance. Little happens without reference to some sort of **timetable**. The need for timetables started in the nineteenth century when the first big factories were built and it became important for people to work together under one roof. People no longer worked according to the seasons and the natural rhythms of the day. Today, our lives are organized so that people arrive at and leave schools, factories, or offices at set times, all year round.

Good Timing

We use time to make life easier. Busy roads, for example, would come to a standstill without timed traffic lights. At busy intersections, traffic from one direction is given time to clear before cars from another direction are allowed to cross. The timing of the traffic lights is set so that no one has to wait too long, and it can vary according to the time of day.

Twenty-Four-Hour Clocks

To avoid confusion, transportation timetables are arranged using the twenty-four-hour system of time. Usually, we divide the day into two parts, each having twelve hours. We put **a.m.** (short for the Latin *ante meridiem*, which means "before noon") or **p.m.** (*post meridiem*, which means "after noon") after the time to tell us if the hour is in the morning or the afternoon. This clock (*right*) shows the time as a twenty-four-hour period in which a.m. and p.m. are not used. The hours continue past twelve to twenty-four. Therefore, 06:00 is six o'clock a.m., and 18:00 is six o'clock p.m.

Clocking In

Are you a slave to time? Time has become so important to us that it is even used to keep track of people. Factories always have had methods of "clocking in and out." Workers usually register the time they arrive at and leave the factory by putting a card into a machine attached to a clock.

TV Times

TV and radio guides are timetables that are published in newspapers and magazines. They are arranged so that people can see the times of the programs at a glance and plan their night's viewing with ease. You can set a video recorder to record a TV program at a particular time so you don't miss it.

Winding Down

In a clock, when the coiled spring that provides the power becomes slack, the clock slows down and eventually stops. This process is called "winding down." To make the clock work again, the spring must be tightened or wound up. Similarly, we use the phrase "winding down" when we forget our busy timetables and begin to relax. And we often say we are "wound up" when we feel tense or anxious.

Called to Prayer

People do not always rely on clocks and watches to keep to their timetables. Muslims are called to prayer by an official, called a muezzin, from the minaret of the mosque where they worship. In Christian countries, some churches ring bells to announce the times of services. In Israel, a siren heralds the start of the Jewish Sabbath at sunset on Fridays.

Making Connections

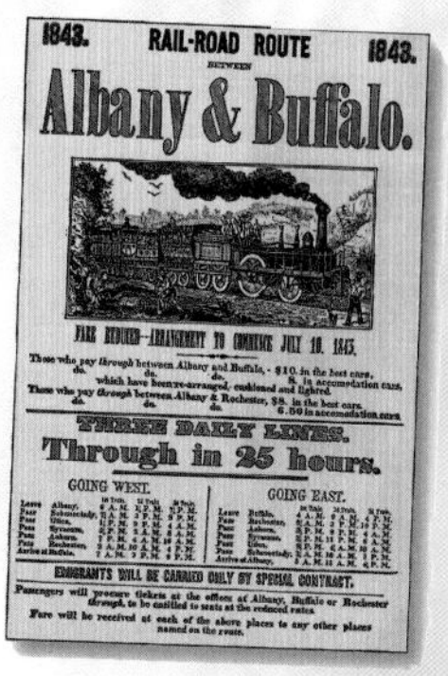

Timetables are essential for planning trips. They tell us when buses, trains, or airplanes depart and help us make connections between them. Timetables became important in the nineteenth century when they were widely used by the new railroad companies to advertise their services. By knowing when the trains would run, passengers could plan their travels well in advance.

Keeping the World on Time

As Earth spins, some parts of the world are in sunlight while others are in darkness. When it is midday in New York, for example, it is midnight in Australia. Because it is impossible to set the same time for every part of the world, each area has its own local time according to when the Sun rises and sets. Consequently, the world has been divided into time zones, which are regions of Earth within which the same time is used. There are twenty-four time zones, reflecting the twenty-four hours of the day. As Earth turns a complete 360 degrees in a day, each time zone covers fifteen degrees. The Bureau International de l'Heure in Paris coordinates the world's time signals. It uses atomic clocks to send out signals that are accurate to a millisecond.

The Prime Meridian

Since 1884, the world has measured its time from the **prime meridian**, which runs through Greenwich in London. A meridian is an imaginary **line of longitude** that runs from the North Pole to the South Pole. Greenwich is at zero degrees longitude, and the local time there is known as Greenwich mean time (GMT) or universal time (UT). As you move west and cross fifteen degrees of longitude, you move into a new time zone and must set your watch back one hour. Conversely, as you move east, you must set your watch ahead.

John Harrison and the H4

John Harrison, the inventor of the H1 clock, pursued his quest to win a prize awarded to the inventor of a clock that found longitude to within half a degree (equal to two minutes of time). Such a clock could not lose or gain more than three seconds in twenty-four hours. Harrison's H4 watch (*left*) was tested on a voyage to the West Indies in 1761–1762. It lost only five seconds during the journey, which meant the navigator could figure out where he was on a map with an accuracy of less than .6 mile (1 km).

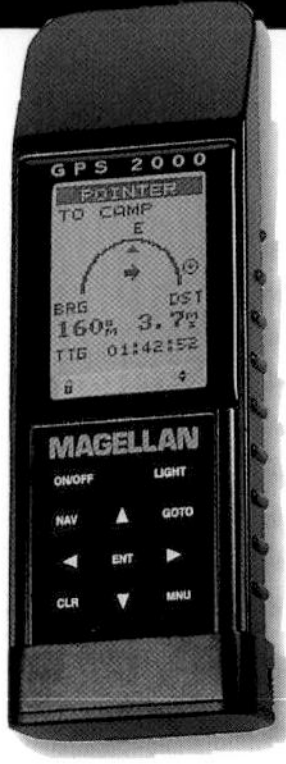

Global Positioning Systems (GPS)

Modern methods of finding longitude and **latitude** have changed navigation. Satellite navigation, or NAVSAT, has helped ships' crews and airline pilots for more than twenty years. With GPS devices (*left*), sailors can find both positions and directions anywhere in the world to within .6 mile (1 km).

NAVSTAR

NAVSTAR (NAVigation System using Time And Ranging) is the satellite system at the heart of satellite navigation technology. As a NAVSTAR satellite (*right*) orbits Earth, it sends out signals that can be picked up by GPS devices (*far left*).

No Landmarks at Sea

An old sailing ship navigated with the help of an accurate clock called a chronometer. Out in the open ocean, there were no landmarks to help identify a ship's position. With an accurate clock set to GMT, sailors could find how far east or west they were (their longitude) from the prime meridian. To find their latitude, they used the angle of the Sun during the day and certain stars at night. Their position on the ocean was the point where the lines of longitude and latitude met.

Time Zones of the World

Long journeys by plane often result in jet lag. People develop a general feeling of physical and mental tiredness because their body clocks are out of step with a new time zone. The time difference between England and New York is five hours. but the journey takes about seven hours. If you took off from London at lunchtime, you would arrive in New York only two hours later. Your body clock, however, would tell you it was dinnertime. It takes a body clock a few days to adjust to a new time zone.

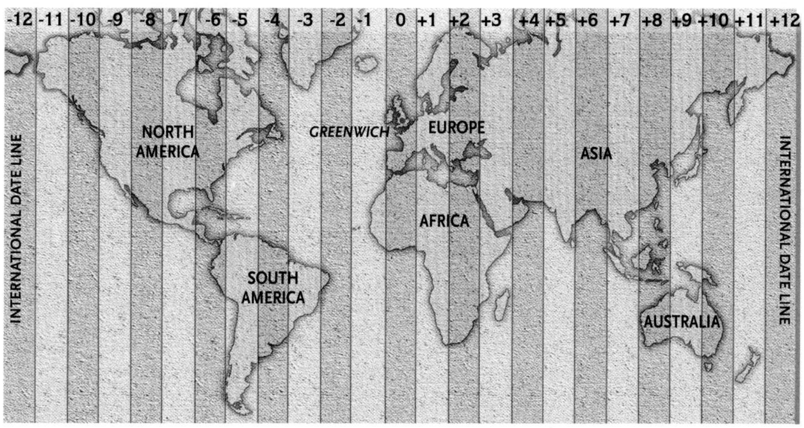

Looking Back in Time

History gives meaning to our lives and also can give us a sense of identity. Evidence of the past is all around us. We find it in written documents, paintings and photographs, buildings, historical artifacts, and even our own memories. We can use these historical records to draw pictures of the past, to put events into a neat sequence or chronological order. We can draw time lines that show the significance of the events and the effects they have had. This organization of the past helps us make sense of changes and determine the way we may be going in the future.

Natural Logbooks

Trees are the longest-living things on Earth. Every year a tree lays down a growth ring, which represents one year on a time line. Cross sections of very old trees have hundreds of growth rings. If you know when the tree was cut down, you can link its rings with great events in history. When the weather is dry, trees do not grow much, and the growth ring is narrow. When the weather is good for growth, the ring is wide. Scientists have used this information to discover what the climate of an area was like, even in ancient times.

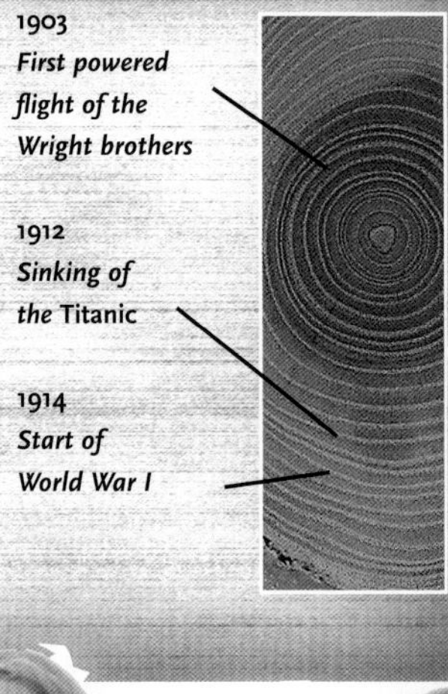

Life Span

A life span is an amount of time that a living thing or a machine may be expected to live or work. Every living thing has its own life span. People have life spans of approximately seventy-five years, and some tortoises may live for 150 years, but trees can live for centuries, even **millennia**.

Changing Fashions

We often date things according to what was in fashion during a particular **decade**. People think of the 1960s, for example, as "the swinging sixties." Skirts were short, hair was long, the music of groups such as the Beatles was a driving force in society, and many long-held beliefs went through radical change.

Wars and Revolutions

Le Petit Parisien
ÉDITION DE PARIS
JEUDI 12 NOVEMBRE 1942

Adolf Hitler ordonne à ses troupes d'assurer la protection du littoral méditerranéen et de la Corse

LE FÜHRER EXPLIQUE SES DÉCISIONS IMPOSÉES PAR L'AGRESSION ANGLO-AMÉRICAINE DANS DEUX MESSAGES AU MARECHAL PÉTAIN ET AU PEUPLE FRANÇAIS

LE MESSAGE AU PEUPLE FRANCAIS

Il a offert au Chef de l'État, ainsi qu'au gouvernement, la possibilité de se rendre à Versailles et de circuler librement dans tout le territoire

Je formule l'espoir, a-t-il ajouté, que ces mesures prises amènent un rapprochement entre les peuples européens. L'Allemagne est par conséquent décidée à défendre, si possible côte à côte avec les soldats français, les frontières de votre pays

LA LETTRE AU MARECHAL

Wars have a dramatic effect on people's lives, so when people look back in history, they may refer to a war to describe a particular time. Historians often divide the twentieth century into the years of World War I (1914–1918) and World War II (1939–1945) and the periods before, between, and after them. Revolutions are times of great change within a country, so these, too, are often used to mark periods of history. The Russian Revolution (1917), for example, saw the establishment of a communist government in Russia. The Industrial Revolution (1760–1830) changed Europe and the United States from rural to industrial societies.

The Computer Age

Periods in history that are marked by some important feature are often given a special name, such as "the computer age." We now take personal computers for granted, but just forty years ago, they existed only in people's fantasies. Computers now are used everywhere, which is why the "millennium bug" frightened people as the year 2000 approached. Many computers needed their internal clocks reset to recognize the date 2000 — the millennium year.

Kings and Queens

Historians often name distinctive periods after the kings, queens, or presidents who were in power at the time. "Elizabethan," for example, is a term used to describe the period when Elizabeth I was Queen of England (1558–1603). Her reign was notable for commercial growth and flourishing arts. Another example is the "Reagan years," the period (1981-1989) when Ronald Reagan was president of the United States.

Time Gone By

We all remember what it was like when we were younger — the toys we had, the games we played, our time at school. These same memories differ in each generation. The memories of an elderly person will be entirely different from those of someone twenty or thirty years younger.

Geological Time

Humans have been on Earth for only a comparatively short period of time. If the history of the world were compared to a twenty-four-hour period, humans would appear only in the last few seconds before midnight. So how can scientists tell how Earth was formed hundreds of millions of years before people existed? One way is to date rocks by measuring the small amounts of radioactivity in them. When the rocks were formed, radioactive elements were trapped inside. These elements slowly give out energy at a known rate, enabling scientists to calculate the date the rocks formed. The time scale that shows these important events in Earth's history is called the geological record.

Ice Ages

Landscapes with deep, U-shaped, steep-sided valleys, such as in the Alps, in Europe, provide dramatic evidence of the Ice Ages long past. The great weight of huge rivers of ice, hundreds of feet thick, pressed down on the valley floors. Rocks and boulders trapped in the ice acted like sandpaper as the ice pushed forward, forming the features of the land we see today.

Grand Canyon

The Colorado River has cut deeply into the land, forming a famous gorge known as the Grand Canyon. The layers of rock in this picture of the Grand Canyon (*right*) were once moving sand and mud on the bottom of a sea. Over millions of years, the sand and mud dried and hardened into mudstone and sandstone many feet thick.

Ancient Trees

Bristlecone pines (*left*), which grow on the slopes of the Rocky Mountains in the western United States, are among the oldest-living trees in the world. Some bristlecone pines are five thousand years old. They were seedlings before the pyramids were built in Egypt.

Carbon Dating

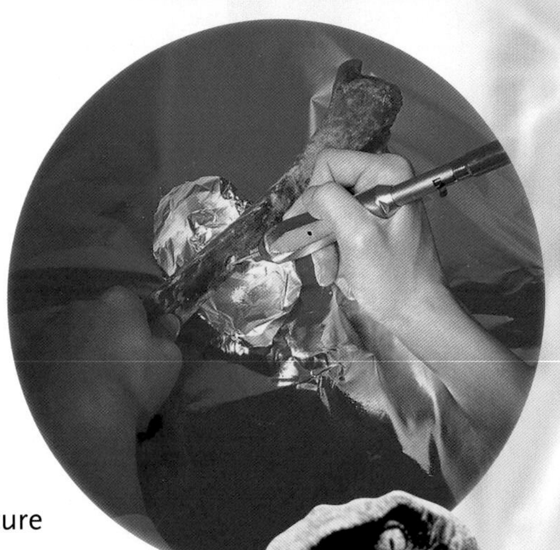

Carbon is the basis of life. It is found in every tissue of all the animals and plants that ever lived. Scientists have discovered that one particular form of carbon, called carbon 14, is absorbed by a living thing only while that organism is still alive. Carbon 14 gives off tiny amounts of radioactivity. When a creature dies, this radioactivity gets weaker and weaker in a process called radioactive decay. By discovering how weak the decay has become, scientists can determine how long ago the creature lived. This piece of reindeer bone (*right*) is being prepared for **carbon dating**.

The Fossil Record

Fossils are the dead remains of animals and plants that have been embedded in rocks and preserved for millions of years. By studying fossils, geologists can tell what early creatures, such as dinosaurs, looked like. By dating the rocks, they discover when the creatures lived. Prehistoric time is divided into stages called eras, which are subdivided into periods. Scientists can date these periods according to the ages of the fossils they find.

Evolutionary Time

Geologists think that Earth is 4,550 million years old and that the earliest forms of life appeared 3,500 million years ago. There is evidence that modern humans, people like ourselves, lived in Africa about 100,000 years ago, but establishing the theory of how humans evolved from apes has been difficult because the few fossilized remains have been widely scattered.

On Earth, a mile or a kilometer is a good way to measure long distances, but such quantities don't work to describe the huge spaces between the stars. We need another, more manageable, way to measure distances in the universe. Scientists came up with a clever term for measuring the vastness between the stars, and it involves time — the **light-year**. Light travels incredibly fast — about 186,000 miles (300,000 km) a second — which is about 5.88 trillion miles (9.46 trillion km) a year. That distance is a very long way, but, in the emptiness of space, a light-year is relatively short. Our galaxy, the Milky Way, is about 1,500 light-years thick at the center and 150,000 light-years across.

Absolute Time

Isaac Newton (1642–1727) thought time flowed at the same rate for everyone, no matter where they were. He called this "absolute time," and he believed that, throughout the universe, everyone and everything must be at the same moment of "now." Newton also discovered rules, or laws, on which the universe runs. These laws explained, for the first time, how the planets and stars moved. Newton saw the universe as a giant clockwork machine, with everything working predictably. Newton's ideas were unchallenged for two hundred years.

Relativity

In 1905, Albert Einstein (1879–1955) came up with totally new ways of explaining how the universe worked. These ideas were included in his theory of special relativity, and they showed that strange things happen when objects move at very high speeds. Moving clocks, for example, run slower than clocks that are standing still. In 1916, Einstein also came up with a description of how the universe works in his general theory of relativity, which was a theory of gravity that also predicted an expanding universe.

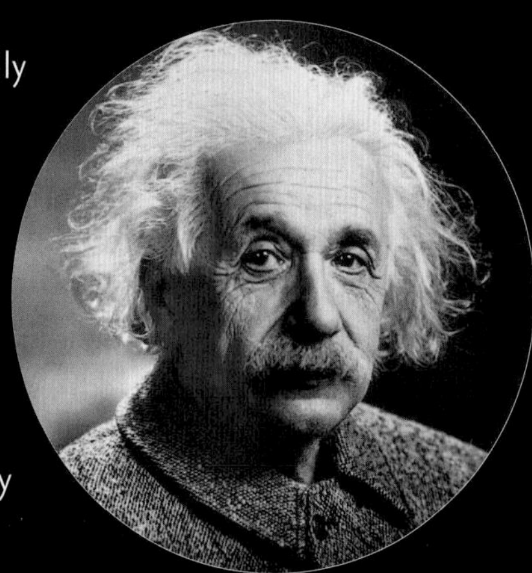

The Beginning of Time

The **Big Bang** is a theory that explains the origins of the universe. It claims that all the stuff of the universe once was held in a single, incredibly dense state. Then, in a huge explosion, matter was hurled out in all directions, forming the galaxies, stars, and planets we see today. By studying the universe's rate of expansion, astronomers concluded that the Big Bang took place about twelve billion years ago.

Into the Past

The spectacular Eagle Nebula is a cloud of particles and gases seven thousand light-years away from Earth. This picture (*right*) shows what the Eagle Nebula looked like seven thousand years ago. It has taken that long for the light to reach Earth. Whenever we look up at the night sky, we really are looking back into the past. We do not know what is happening right now in the huge vastness of space because the light has not reached us yet!

Time on Jupiter

If we lived on Jupiter, our days and years would be very different. Jupiter is the giant planet of the solar system. It is more than three hundred times the size of Earth. Despite its size, it spins very fast, making a day (and night) just ten hours long. While Earth takes one year to go around the Sun, Jupiter takes twelve years. The length of a day and a year are different for every planet in the solar system.

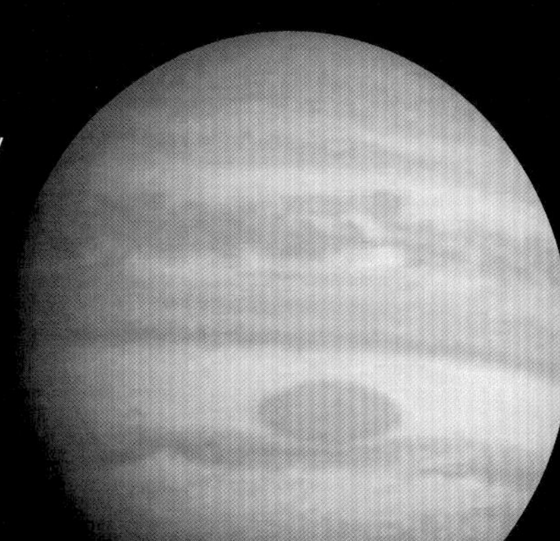

The Fourth Dimension

What is time? Where does time go? Time appears to move at different speeds according to what we are doing. When we are bored, time seems to drag; when we are enjoying ourselves, time seems to fly. Time is "slippery" because it cannot be pinned down or held like an object, but it always goes in one direction, like an arrow pointing from the past into the future. But what if time was not like that? What if the time that we use was not lost forever? Or what if we could jump backward and forward through time? If time suddenly reversed itself, clocks would run backward, birds would fly backward, and people would grow young instead of old! Thinking of time as a fourth dimension is a topic for science fiction, but is it all make-believe? Only time will tell.

Defying Time

Will it ever be possible to defy time? Since ancient times, many people have claimed to know the secrets of eternal youth. Creams, cosmetics, diets, and even surgery promise to make us look younger, but, like all past methods, they will not keep us from dying of old age. Scientists are beginning to unlock the secrets of the aging process and may discover a way to live longer — but not forever. Some people think that future technology will allow them to live longer, so they choose to be frozen when they die, using a technique called **cryogenics**. More bizarre is the story of Jeremy Bentham (*left*) who, in 1832, willed his body to medical science on the condition that his skeleton be dressed in his own clothes with a wax likeness of his face. Bentham still sits, greeting visitors, at University College in London.

Changing History

Traveling into the past seems like a wonderful idea. You could warn the captain of the *Titanic* that he should change course to avoid the iceberg that will sink his ship. If you did that, hundreds of passengers who died might have lived. Many families, however, would now be different. Perhaps you would never have been born. Then how could you warn the captain? Nothing is straightforward when considering time as the fourth dimension.

The Fourth Dimension

We often hear about time as the fourth dimension added to the three dimensions of space (height, width, and depth) that give objects form and shape. It is as if time and space are two different things. Space is the expanse in which we move around, whereas time is something we move with or through. According to Einstein, however, space and time are not separate but are joined together in a single entity called space-time. They exist only together, and you could not have one without the other.

Time Travel

Films such as *Back to the Future* and *Bill and Ted's Excellent Adventure* play with the idea of time travel, but is time travel possible? Scientists believe **black holes** could be the key. Black holes are stars that have collapsed in on themselves. Their gravity is so strong that not even light can escape. If you fall through a black hole, you might end up in another time and place. The universe you would end up in might not be the one you started from. There may be many different universes all linked together by lots of different black holes.

More Information

When the Gregorian calendar was introduced in Britain in 1752, there were riots in the streets.
When the government finally decided to adopt Pope Gregory XIII's calendar, solving the error of a missing day every 128 years, special arrangements were made to make the adjustment go smoothly. The government announced that September 2 would be followed by September 14, creating a loss of eleven days. Ordinary people, however, thought their lives had been shortened and they were losing days of wages, so they rioted, shouting, "Give us back our eleven days!"

Scientists used atomic clocks to prove that moving clocks run slower than stationary clocks.
Atomic clocks were used in the experiment because they are incredibly accurate. One clock was flown around the world, and its time was compared with a clock left on the ground. The difference was measured in billionths of a second, enough to prove that time slows down as predicted by Einstein's theory.

Albert Einstein, the man who revolutionized our ideas of time and space, became so involved in his thoughts that he would lose track of time.
Rather than making scientific discoveries by carrying out practical experiments, Einstein thought out all of his theories about time and space in his head. Often he would go for a walk, and he would be so caught up in his imagination that he would wander for hours, totally unaware of what time it was!

Some astronomers have predicted that time and space may end with a big crunch.
Millions of years from now, the universe may stop expanding and start to collapse. It is possible that the galaxies will shrink and form black holes. At the final moment, all the black holes would merge, sucking all the remaining matter of the universe into one large black hole, destroying time and space. It also is possible that a new Big Bang may follow the big crunch, creating a new cycle of Creation.

Web Sites

A Walk through Time
physics.nist.gov/GenInt/Time/time.html
Learn more about how the measurement of time evolved.

Nova: Einstein's Big Idea
www.pbs.org/wgbh/nova/einstein/
Find out the story behind the world's biggest equation.

Standard Time Zone Chart of the World
www.worldtimezone.com
Get information about the time of day all over the world.

a.m. — the abbreviation for *ante meridiem* (before noon)
atomic clock — a clock that uses the energy change that takes place in atoms to keep track of time
Big Bang — a theory of the origin of the universe
black hole — a star that has collapsed into itself and has such strong gravity that not even light can escape
body clock — a built-in sense of time
carbon dating — figuring out the age of something by its carbon 14 content
circadian rhythm — a pattern of waking and sleeping based on the length of the day and the night
clepsydra — a clock that uses water to measure time
cryogenics — a technique for freezing a dead body in hopes of resuscitating it at a future time
decade — a time period of ten years
dimension — a measurement in one direction, such as height, width, or depth
generation — a measurement of the time it takes for children to grow up and become parents
geological record — the time scale that uses the geology of Earth to mark important events in the history of Earth
Gregorian calendar — the calendar we use today that had three fewer leap years every four hundred years than the Julian calendar
hibernating — spending cold winter months in a resting state in which body temperature drops and all physical functions slow down
hourglass — a glass vessel with two compartments for measuring time. One is filled with sand that trickles through a small opening to fill the other one in a specific amount of time.
Julian calendar — the calendar established by Julius Caesar with twelve months and a leap year every four years
latitude — an imaginary line extending east and west around the globe to indicate how far north or south a place is from the Poles or the equator
leap year — a year when February has 29 days
light-year — the distance that light travels in one year: 5.88 trillion miles (9.46 trillion km)
line of longitude — an imaginary line extending north and south around the globe to indicate how far east or west a place is from the prime meridian
lunar month — the time it takes for the Moon to complete an orbit around Earth (about 29.5 days)
metronome — a device that produces a rhythmical clicking sound to help musicians keep time
migration — a seasonal traveling of birds or other animals
millennia — time periods of one thousand years
pendulum — a weight that swings from a fixed point
perennial plants — plants that live more than one year
p.m. — the abbreviation for *post meridiem* (after noon)
prime meridian — an imaginary line extending north and south through Greenwich, England, designated as zero degrees longitude. The prime meridian registers Greenwich mean time (GMT) or universal time (UT).
quartz — a mineral that vibrates at a constant frequency when placed in an electric field
solar year — the time it takes for Earth to go around the Sun: about 365.25 days
synchronize — set clocks to arrange events to happen at the same time
time zone — areas of Earth where the people set their clocks to the same time
timetable — a schedule showing a planned order or sequence of events based on times they occurred or will occur

Index